Gallery Books
Editor: Peter Fallon

BARNSLEY MAIN SEAM

Pearse Hutchinson

BARNSLEY
MAIN SEAM

Gallery Books

Barnsley Main Seam
is first published
simultaneously in paperback
and in a clothbound edition
on 30 March 1995.

The Gallery Press
Loughcrew
Oldcastle
County Meath
Ireland

ISBN 1 85235 155 1 (*paperback*)
1 85235 156 X (*clothbound*)

The Gallery Press receives financial assistance from An Chomhairle
Ealaíon / The Arts Council, Ireland.

Contents

for Alan Biddle
(Kircubbin 1952-Dublin 1994)

A Memory of Belfast in 1974

for Caoimhe Ní Dhuibhinn

The towering menace-aforethought
imperial-metal contraption the people named
Silver City no sheepswool stuck
in its high wire that Sunday morning,
and the warm sky wasn't bleeding.
But under the menace, on the grass,
children were playing.
Some o' them swinging on new bright-coloured swings,
swinging right up to the sky,
their small feet almost reaching Silver City,
almost toppling it down.

It wasn't the Sabbath-authorities put the swings there,
but the Lord's Day did its bit to barb the wire.

Three of us strolling, that sunny morning,
it nearly felt like peace.

Then we were stopped for questioning.
Nowt serious, it didn't last long,
but as we resumed our stroll
the oldest of us said:

'I'm 61.
I was born in this city,
I've lived here all my life,
an' I can't go for a walk on a Sunday morning
without being stopped by a British soldier.'

The sun was dazzling on Silver City
as back we strolled for Sunday dinner,
the swings were still — the kids
must all have gone home for theirs.

Before we got back to his house
he stopped and said to me:
'We're a betrayed people' —
looking me straight in the eyes,
like a Cree Indian telling it like it is
to the soi-disant-white camera:
'We're a betrayed people.'

Later we sat drinking beer in the back garden.
The helicopters with their ugly blurting
only attacked the blue sky
every fifteen minutes,
but at times they came quite low.

The Right to Love

for Mairéad Looby

A young woman in the Bogside went out walking
with a British Tommy, so the freedom-fighters
tarred-and-feathered her — before that torture
did English conscript and Irish girl make love?
go the whole hog? let's hope they did
for what's it to anyone whether or no
's goidé sin don té sin nach mbaineann sin dó
but the freedom-fighters said it was
their business, called her a risk, a threat
but her mother cried out:
Wee girls have a right to love!
crying out from her heart
who was once a wee girl herself
crying out from her loving heart
for all the world to hear
crying out to a world of love beyond
even her own people's agony and hope
even beyond her own, but yet within
all such hope, all suffering —
her shriek of hope
making its dogged, quiet way
through all the conventional, fashionable,
holier-than-thou, halfways-liberal newsprint
to lovers everywhere,
to pity poor lovers everywhere:
Wee girls have a right to love.

She Fell Asleep in the Sun

'She fell asleep in the sun.'

That's what they used to say
in South Fermanagh
of a girl who gave birth
unwed.

A woman from Kerry told me
what she'd always heard growing up was
leanbh ón ngréin:
a child from the sun.

And when a friend of mine from Tiernahilla
admired in North Tipperary
a little lad running round a farmyard
the boy's granda smiled:
'garsúinín beag mishtake'.

A lyrical ancient kindliness
that could with Christ accord.
Can it outlive technolatry?
or churches?

Not to mention that long, leadránach,
latinate, legal, ugly
twelve-letter name not
worthy to be called a name,
that murderous obscenity — to call

any child ever born
that excuse for a name
could quench the sun for ever.

Let's Hope

A girl and her child
extinct in a field.
A boy got beaten to death in a park.
They didn't mean to kill him.
They live.
His family say he wasn't.
Nobody meant to kill her.
One morning last year
from the top deck of a bus
I saw the living sunlight flooding
trees and grass in Fairview Park
with light, life, splendour —
as if no death,
as if no hate,
as if no ignorance ever.
Perhaps that very same morning filled
her field of death with glory —
even love: some sort.
Whether he was or not, let's hope
he enjoyed whatever it was,
or just himself, before
they taught themselves
no lesson soon enough.
Let's hope Ann Lovett knew,
before that fear, some joy.

Until

een fenster is alles
        — Paul van Ostaijen

The way an old man from his window looks out at the beauty
        of nature
                    grass, trees, creatures
                        the beauty surviving the horror
is not the same way that a young man
        looks out the window and goes out the door and enters
his own full nature and every nature and goes on living them all
        crushed insect, predator's prey: not surviving, not surviving
but the young man still living it all
        living it up and living through it all
                dancing or crawling every minute of it until
                    he sits looking out of a window

Snowflake

for Richard Riordan

Snowflake in a spider's web
sycamore-leaf in a bay-tree.

Filament clung to the back
window for days that winter,
keeping the snowflake, never
a spider in sight, each morning
for days I looked and still
the snowflake held in the web
as pure a white
as when it first came down —
all other snow
well gone — then rain
washed away that flake.

From a tall tree last autumn
one tawny leaf wind-crossed
the front garden, came to rest
in close-clustering dark-green
bay just under a window
unseason sheltering season
for a few days. For days:
the big, five-point, mottlegolden
leaf in dark-green held
while sycamore-leaf upon leaf
went underfoot in grass.

Bringing back
a snowflake.

May 1989

An Empty House

The small sycamore
invading the bird-house
thrusting those
unmistakable, beautiful
big leaves
into the kennel-like
dark emptiness
the birdless
even crumbless
blank space
filling
with living
green.

The bird-house
began in the back.
No birds entered,
tho' once a tiny
bird with a blue tail
alighted on
the roof a split
second. Shunted
to the front garden —
less cat-risk —
the bird-house
still failed.

Soon again
the small invading
tree will be
trimmed back,
the desolate kennel
still ignored
by small birds
feeding on the grass.

Saturnino

for Jürgen Dierking

Hurling the frail door wide open, erupting down
from dim-lit narrow side-street three shallow steps
into the dark, small, quiet pub the raw young marine
in dark blue blared
'Is there nobody here?'
where Ernie and I were percht on stools at the counter
getting slowly sozzled conversing with Saturnino
the half-tipsy publican from León
who didn't know, just as well, what the gringo said
but Ernie knew exactly what the young lad meant
so 'Further down the Ramblas' he said gesturing lavishly,
his blond beard curling with amusement,
naming a dive where every sixth-fleet lecher
could rapidly get laid,
the lad scooted away
and Saturnino enquired: 'What did he say?'

When we told him, he got very angry:
we were the only three people in the pub,
but we were there
we were three
we were people
'Are we nobody?' he cried (tho' not in English)
rushing out along the narrow street
but came back fast from the Ramblas so loud and bright
Three brandies on the house, cheap rotgut stuff but still
'Are we not people?' he cried, at least three times
(at times only the literal
can express the imagination,
achieve any generous truth)
and then he erupted again in even greater anger
thinking of the women who'd have to be kind to that
        unthinking boy,

the women of his town, the women from all over Spain,
so he rushed to the door again and flung it wide
and cried into the narrow, dark, empty street:
'Con la gana que tienen
                              las pobres mujeres!
With the hunger they have — those poor women!
Con la *gana* que *tien*en
                              las *pob*res mu*jer*es!'
More than one of whom often
patronized his pub.
Drink was dirt-cheap in those days,
tho' the whores were beginning to get dear:
las pobres
            pobres mujeres
con la gana que tienen
con la gana those poor women
who were people
who were many
who were there.

Deprivation, Luxury, Envy

A man and a boy standing side by side
gazing into a cake-shop window
a posh Konditorei on a posh boulevard
the man lacking the money for even a cheap drink
who knows perhaps the boy could have bought the man
a glass of rotgut brandy
but a cake in that shop could cost the earth
the boy looked underfed not even enough lentils
let alone a posh cake.

Man and boy stood side by side for long minutes
without a word, the boy never once looking
at the man even out of the corner of his eye
The man wanted to say to the boy
I get paid next week I could buy you a few cakes
but he hadn't the courage so they went on standing there
side by side not speaking not making common cause
just eaten up with envy
the posh cakes eating their hearts away.

Then the boy walked off. And the man,
lacking the courage to break the window,
made for the nearest non-boulevardier bar,
where if the right member of the family was on
he might get a little more credit.

Even when at last he got paid
it wasn't to that shop the man went for cakes.
That city was chock-full of cake-shops.

Odessa

Called a Jew
six times:
once in middle age
five times in youth

Drunk Dublinmen
four times
as an insult
in pubs
but a courteous Dutchman
by water
in Haarlem

From '44 to '46
four times in Dublin pubs:
You're a Yid
        I'm not
You look like a Yid
           I'm not
You're a dirty Yid
         I'm not
         but I wish I was
You're a fuckin' Yid
        I am
        so what?

That last time
and the second-last
I was really frightened:
both men nearly hit me
only Dutch courage
(as a coward called it)
had at last made
indignation brave

One day in '52
walking in utter quiet
along the bank of a sunny canal in Haarlem
I lost my way
and bridge after bridge
not a soul in sight
no one even sitting on a stoep;
with a train to catch
I began to panic
then heaven sent
a very small old man
walking slowly in front of me

white hair, black suit,
small wizened face
not a word of English
he'd see me on my way
but he walked so slow!
Gij bent een Jied, he said
I knew that must be slang
but Why? said I
De baard, said he: the beard

After a pause:
There used to be thousands of them here
before the war
many in kaftans
The Germans took them away
After another pause:
They never did us any harm
not that I could see

Then our ways parted
I shook his hand and thanked him

I could have hugged him
I should have kissed and hugged him
hugged his frail old body
his true Dutch courage and courtesy
No one ever again called me a Jew
save that a Jewish friend in Leeds in '73
after six months of trust said:
I thought at first you might be Jewish
not because of your nose
but because of your lip — he smiled
so I smiled too, a trifle bravely
(and to think that my Seville Place father,
who spoke with affection of Odessa
and of Clanbrassil Street
used to call it a Hapsburg lip)

Those Dublin bowsies at the war's end,
all middle-aged, none well-heeled,
went for the nose not the lip.
That small old man in Haarlem,
by sunlit, peaceful water,
didn't look well-heeled either.

Ostfriesland

for Theo Schuster

1

I'm eating with four Germans
in a small East-Friesian town
magnificent Italian food.
Our host, a gallant man
who keeps on bringing out
books and records in the Nahsprachen —
tongues near to German —
for example: Plattdütsch.
And,
     for example,
              Yiddish.

He tells us, over
the sumptuous food,
there lives here now
only one Jew.
For a wild second I wonder
is it him?

Earlier, in his bookshop, leafing through
a history of this town,
I found a synagogue-photo.

Built in the 1880s. Burnt down,
like so many,
on Kristallnacht.

Now at the Italian table
I remember that small picture,
and wonder.

But imagine it,
that one Jewish man
going back there, after the war —
after that war —
coming back (from where?)
coming back to what had been
his town too,
to make it, perhaps, his town again,
to be, in a way, alone there.

I fall silent, we all do
for a minute.
What right have I to wonder
or imagine?
Common humanity?
What right to assume it was ever
his town? Or doubt it?

2

One of these four I'm eating with
is the friend who brought me here,
a poet who has railed against and mocked
all hatred and savagery.
Two are sisters,
charming and beautiful,
who fed me as well as Italians could
on a balcony under the warm night
a week ago in Bremen.

I remember Elie Cohen the Dutch rabbi
telling the Dutch, after that war:
Don't think it couldn't happen here,

it could happen anywhere,
even in Holland.

3

Isroel
not ah but oh
not Israel but Isroel — that so
surprising vowel that unexpected *o*
sounding out clear on the LP sent — as good as his word —
to me in Bloom's town (whether his, or mine)
from a small East-Friesian town
sounding out in the rich prose
of a great storyteller Itschak Leib Peretz
in the rich voice
of Zvi Hofer
of the Institutum Judaicum
of Münster — Leib Peretz
who spoke with passion for Yiddish to be
the national tongue of the nation-to-be
Isroel

Peretz
lost out to Hebrew, but on this record
made in Germany, not anywhere else,
his passion speaks again, his vivid zest,
all that humour and variety
which even goyim can tell (with the aid
of certain famous books) all that life
defying oppression, prejudice, all the narrowing forces,
abounds again, speaks Yiddish again, in Zvi
Hofer's abundant voice
as rich as Hebrew itself.

Winters

The old in winter
longing for the spring
hating the cold
longing for the first warm days
as if
wishing their lives away
even sooner

People at work
longing for pay-day
as if wishing
their lives away

People out-of-work
longing for dole-day
as if wishing —

And all wish
the very opposite:
more life, not less!

Workers
hating the 12-month winter
of low pay
The workless
hating their 12-month winter

The old in winter
shivering over heaters
longing for the spring

The horse lies
half out of the icy lake
its wings frozen

Barnsley Main Seam

for Peter Kiddle

Impeccable snow, eternally fresh, gold-clustering —
limitless icefield sparkled with golden igloos,
an ordered sprinkling, all mathematics
made sumptuous like the sound
of Ceva's theorem — the whole ceiling
so boundless a roof so soaring
as almost babellious in its worship,
                              Vatican-voluptuous,
higher than God's own sky,
higher and whiter than even serenest
clouds over the Brecklands. Look! look up
at us, honey-knobs, pommes mousseline:
perfection of man's making —

Yet for-all-that a feast, a true an even chaste
feast for spirit as for eye —
Stefansdom, Gaudí —
and for-all-that more accessible
to the tiny floored nape craning up
(like Capek flat on his back in the pocked Alhambra)
than the Five Grey Sisters:
                              grey-stained infinite-oblong glass,
austerest glass, how rich a grey,
an almost velvet grey, bleak brocade,
stuff so harsh hauteur
                              you'd never want to stroke,
noli-me-tangere-vaginistic charm —
and flat on his back forever
the lissome silvery armour-body of young Prince William,
only thirteen, poor mite,
endless gazing sightless up
at buttertub slobs in a muslin-spud expanse,
no Amsterdancing prinsiade now for him,

his long grey slim steel as graced
as the five giant Sisters but him stretched

only one young boy, not five pious bayonets,
just one dead boy who never chose
to be born a prince but perhaps more easily
forgot he didn't
                    than
the miners who made the timber model
of Barnsley Main Seam

Not of high stone
not of deep coal
not of gold snow
nor grey glass
they built their small model
nestling modest into the minster wall:
'The Tribute of the Yorkshire Miners
to the Minster' —
or so it says and there the little model men are
not in sumptuous colours woven
not in bleak brocade
but well worked in wood
working away at the coal-face —

A hunk of white bread, spattered in blood,
and a black rag, aloft on a pike:
the hungry women of Honiton made their protest clear.
But that was in the bad old days, long before
enlightened centuries when the milk-thief drove
Derby and Merthyr Tydfil to hunger-strike.

Black white and red, those women planting a pike
in high gold-spattered snow
like a dominion flag in a polar icefield:

were *they* in the miners' minds when
they made
and gave
that blunt, matter-of-fact model of a pit-place,
dwarfed by antique splendour,
dwarfing splendour?

Were those riotous women and all the toiling mothers
of miners and masons and all the guilds and all
the muscle called unskilled
back to the tower of Babel and Brú na Bóinne
deep in the miners' minds? as though to say
to all that antique splendour (so buoyant still):
Men like us made you,
without us
you could not be.

Did Primitivo Pérez from
Where the Air is Clear
signing his name in the big book in the narthex
buying a minster minute
observe the miners' tribute, how
clear the sacred air must be
down pit?
Young miners flaunting shoulder-bags in the cage
grinning all over their glad eyes
ready for a prinsiade but
the old honey walls
of York are a different colour entirely —
and is there honey still for tea
in Honiton?
Or black bread, white faces, bad blood?

The Ghost of a Kiss

The two warriors kissing at the ford
after massacring each other all day.
Doctors came with herbs to heal their wounds.
They broke bread together,
that sacred act.
Then they slept,
so as to go on fighting to the death.

At the end of the second day
they kissed again, halfway across the ford.
Which of them was Judas? which Christ?
They had been loving friends.
Herbs were brought. Bread broken.
They slept.

The third night
there was no kissing.
On the fourth day
one killed the other.

The ghost of Judas
cut himself down off his tree,
and ran to the hill to cut down
the ghost of Christ from his.
They embraced, and kissed again,
reliving that other kiss;
but now they had only each other to persecute,
only each other to betray.
They kissed, and started fighting to the death.

British Justice

for Paddy Joe Hill

For British
    read English.
For Justice
    read Law.

Koan

for William Cowper and Umberto Saba

Clearing a kitchen surface too long cluttered
you hear the sound
                    of spent matches
touching the handle of a silver spoon
a gentle tinkle
        you never heard
                that particular
sound before —
il mondo meraviglioso:
there's always a first time

Would unspent matches
lightly driven against
the handle of a silver spoon
make a different sound?

Legend

The Russian word for beautiful
is the Russian word for red.
The Chinese word for silk
is the Chinese word for love.

Beautiful red silk love.

Silk isn't always red —
is love always beautiful?
When you are with me,
yes.

Wouldn't I?

When I'm in your arms, do I think about death?
When I'm in your lovely young arms
I'm far too busy enjoying
being in your arms.
When I'm not in your arms or your company,
that fearful, despicable maniac still
crosses my mind now and then but
almost never stops me in my tracks
bleakly staring as far too often and long
in the ageing decade before
you took me by summer storm.
Let the stern shake their heads, I shan't
get my comeuppance any worse than them;
I never did think much of all
that Eros-Thanatos-inextricable
wisdom of ages. Hubris
has nowt to do with it, it's just
that love's about life not death,
I'm scarcely afraid any more —
tho' when it comes to the point and at my
age it could happen any minute — but in
the meantime and
three years next month is not too bad
as meantimes go tho' here I am
trying to thank you for this in particular and so
for the space of a poem ipso facto mentioning
the bully more often than usual, I wouldn't
go so far as to claim
you've made the wretch irrelevant
but it doesn't seem to matter so much any more,
love can
        work wonders.

Next Time I'll Measure Your Waist

You were so easy and fine last night I scarcely noticed
the homemade halo I'd brought,
rigged-up in a spare dream and you at first
were loath to wear — but I implanted it
firmly just as firm
                              as puritan childhood guilt —
tilt
remorseless tactfully off
your soft black hair

Until you stopped me snoring
                              ('gently', you said gently)
so then I leant across you, nearly falling over,
to look, too eager, under the bed for that ring to snatch back
but it must have melted into the thin ichor
of a spare dream and when you dredged me back
I never missed that half-unreal halo
for the real ring had all its wits about me,
your kind strong body filled us both.

Wooden Hoops for Iron

When Edward Thomas was a child in Wandsworth in the
      Eighties
boys bowled iron hoops
girls
      bowled
            wooden
Were little boys, when iron
fell upon their little bare legs,
better able to stand it?
Erich Fromm, on the other hand,
placed the end of matriarchy at around 1300 B.C.
Before that date did boys and girls both
bowl wooden hoops?
Or girls iron
              and boys wooden?
Some have asserted
the real human rot set in
with the iron age

Delicate wrought-iron balconies
The Gaudiesque torch-extinguishers on a Bath crescent:

But climbing a wooden stile near Saggart
on a now rainy now sunny day
Climbing a wooden stile

But when the Sun was Shining

Too long now since
he stood at the side of a country road,
facing the bushes, watching —
a boy again —
the golden or silver jet
ascending, arching, toppling,
sunlit against no not against but on
the vast blue sky
and then as he fastened up his eyes took in
the whole green countryside
all Ireland his, and every traveller's —

but back to the waiting friends in the patient car
and away again west or south
it wasn't such fun when it rained
and hefted you couldn't wait till the next pub
so facing barbed wire or bushes gone dull
you just let it drizzle
not soaring not sunlit, tho' even then
if the rain too was only drizzle a small
whiskey-bottle you could raise — for even in rain
it shone — up to the skies in defiance,
forgiveness, gratitude, hope

for a break in the distant clouds,
more gorse the further south,
but when the sun was shining that was best,
and you were jetting silver, toppling gold,
claiming the whole green country free to enjoy

February 1992

Sparrowthorn

Remember, Kate, when Sparrowthorn was nearly built
you took me round
               the already attractive house,
and in the bare oblong guest-room-to-be, a bird,
as we stood there halfway
                     between two window-frames
not glazed yet, swiftly flew
                     in-past-us-out, so fast
we barely caught the colour I declare was blue
a plump small bird that for a second flashed
over the bare boards
                   between the bare walls, to clothe
as fabric later — soon — the bare air: a warning
or welcome; who can tell? or no meaning at all
but a blessing, meant or not, as we stood there in the warmth
of friendship and your excitement at this growing home
where children now have grown—
                  how well the bird got through
before the glazier came

early summer, 1989

The Vale of Clara

for Seán and Rosemarie Mulcahy

When the man through the wire fence looked in
    at the young deer beneath the trees
(stopped by its dappled beauty) the surprisingly small animal
    looked at him over its shoulder, then high-stepped away out
        of sight —
how admiration even across so perfect
    a difference can frighten beauty; the man, wondering
whether to feel faintly guilty, christening
    that scruple fatuous, walked along to the gate into the wood.
The trees met high over his head, he walked through, in peace.

Till from the path-side, by his quiet but not quiet enough
    progression disturbed a brace of pheasants clattered
up, clattered away above him, such a loud mad metal clattering
    the man was even more frightened than the small young deer.
He stood still for a minute or two, then not high-stepping
    stepped along regardless.
A narrow, winding stream came down the slope nearly to the path
    its own path faltered by small stones like small weirs, the
        brown
bogwater glinting, flitting in the leafy sunlight,
    the small brown or fawn translucent bubbles forming,
        lingering,
quenching, at the huge pebbles' dalliance —

Three or four bubbles in a tight cluster reminding
    the man of sloe-berries dark bloom but not much glistening
on a slanting bush on a high hill overlooking Glendalough
    climbed up that same September day the dark berries
reminding him then of halfway up that hill sidestepping the
    tight-clustering bright black
sheep-leavings glinting up the hill to the glory of God the Sun.

Bright, light-brown, small water-globes in a wood — the townie
        looked from the high hill down at the round tower
in the pure centre of the valley, ringed — how unerring their choice
        but more meaning for him the visible world
over to the right, off-centre, in the pure middle of a rich meadow
        a spreading oak or elm — school never toyed with nature —
that big tree alone in the centre of a square field.

That big, enduring tree as lovely as all the small
        brief bubbles on a hidden, small wood-stream. This man
                went back
deer-haunted, pheasant-scared, self-scared, contented, cured,
        to the bridge-house of his friends who had given him
that day.

A Wooden Stile

for Garret and Stephen

A wooden stile near Saggart
a now rainy now sunny day
the stile spanned a gate
into the beckoning forest
the small boys climbing over
soon disappeared in the trees
neither one lingered
but the man did
the man who climbed with such
un-boyish care
a few, wet, stile-steps

and then he turned his back on the forest,
turning slow, so
careful not to slip on the wet wood
and looked across at the land sloping away
down to the city and the sea
the lights just beginning to come on

The boys were still in the trees, the man
went on standing on top of a stile and looking.
He knew at last from his care he was middle-ageing
but he didn't care at all — well hardly at all —
for there he was standing on top of a stile and looking
down from as good as a hilltop, if not better —
a wooden stile so simple and clever a man-made thing,
nature and human at ease together, the man would soon
filled with joy but gingerly
descend the four wet steps

And cross the road to his old friends' car,
their two small sons come back from the trees,
and all drive home in friendship.

Font Romeu

You were the burning bush in a barn church,
you were a redsetter leaping
inside my darkest room,
you were never the small faint violet
naked light-bulb in a third-class
hard-bench carriage in a snail-pace train
inside the darkest night, malodorous impossible to read by,
but more the cool green light of a late summer
along the clear-cut sierra the following evening,
your quick saw cut away my lumbering pointless wood,
you were the brightest light on the highest snow at Font
    Romeu,
all my three-tense life
spread out and calming down from that high point:
under your hot-blue naked sky from you, my Pyrenees —
you were never the cliffs of Moher for I could scale you
but more like the whitest foam the sumptuous dark-green sea
down there at the base of the cliff when I was young,
you were never a little white fishbone
prised out of my throat and shining in the penumbra
of an oto-rhino-laryngologist's room the blinds half-drawn
against the unbearable street-heat-light outside,
for you are as neat and far more fair
than even that small white bone and I can swallow you,
I can walk up all your avenues, can bear your heat, your light,
you were the healing water gleaming
in a low-slung, entirely unroman aqueduct
above a dry white-grey riverbed,
you were that sudden red blaze of tomatoes
in one small field in Los Gallardos
in an endless waste of sick-silver esparto famine-dust
where it hadn't rained for eight years,
you were as succulent as Pyrenean pigeon-in-cabbage,
you were the green trees filling the big plain windows —
no lush stained-glass to keep nature out —

of a strictly colourless Hebridean kirk
you were as sudden and rich as the summer trees
breenging in the window the plain pews
pell-mell with rich green leaves
you were the burning bush in a barn church you were and are
all the places I ever travelled to, only truer, only human,
and all the places I never travelled before,
you were the light unerring of the god of youth and love
breaching my darkest cave at the winter solstice.

Pulcherrima Paradigmata

'The sopranos are hard men':
proclaimed in large white
block letters
on a Harcourt St pavement
in the mid-forties:
it lasted for days

In certain dialects of Galician
the word for sister
is the word for brother

'You know,'
said the Virgin Queen
to the Keeper of the Tower,
'that I am Richard the Second'

The Irish
for stallion
is feminine

And as Florence Nightingale
wrote to her Queen,
'I have slept
with some of the finest
women in England.'

Yet Another Reason for Writing in Irish

'He'
is cold,
hard,
weak.

'She'
is warm,
soft,
strong.

An Early Fifties Contrast between the Giudecca and Wexford Street

A tall skinny old woman in a crumpled black-drab
dress right down to her ankles
dancing slow gyrating very slow
all by herself in a big snug
to no music except her own
and all by herself bar me
to no music except the music in her own
head of skimpy every-which-way
grey-white hair

    The long, dull, black dress,
    crumpled,
    I can still see it swaying
    can still see her long, thin,
    utterly pale face,
    flaccid,
    the long thin nose of it,
    the small dark sharp eyes dancing,
    the lively slow swaying
    seventy years of her.

A skinny, less than tall
young man in a drab, crumpled
black smock behind a counter
in a cheap, rudimentary bar,
all by himself when I came in,
his utterly pale, pinched face
shocking in that adriatic summer
between black smock and red, redsetter hair,
his eyes less lively in his twenties
than that old woman's but just as full as hers
but filled with pain and yearning

Small talk, three glasses, growing
unspoken sad-eyed friendship,
'come back tomorrow', but when the young
foreigner went back — behind the counter
only the big brother tough as nails
his dark hair dull his black
smock not crumpled, clean — as hate or pride.

1991

Enriqueta Bru

Everything about her was neat,
and, be sure, still is:
small bones, neat features,
trim figure in trim garb,
fair-to-fawn-to-brown
her neat crisp hair.
She was all clean, with that
iberian, genevese clean-ness
that makes it a lyrical cry.
Shining but calm she was,
her mind like her manners
calmly shining too.

What could she have been — 24?
in the mid-sixties when castilian tyranny
began to thaw, in patches,
deceptive, cat-an'-mouse;
but at last, in some shops,
even in some shop-windows,
books in her native tongue:
la vella plata, the long-
banned speech

we talked in, she and I,
when once a week I came
to that so clean but bleakly clean
crucifyingly un-
lyrical office to put
into the tongue of an even fatter
conqueror than old Castile
a bunch of business-letters for her boss:
black sleeked-back short-
back-an'-sides tight corseted-looking
battleship-dull-dark business suit, civility —

oh such
        sleek bleak civility
(not in our native tongues) he needed me
like a hole in the head I needed him
even less he needed my English bad
I needed his filthy shekels

and so I trudged on sweltering foot
or strap-hanging in jam-packed creaking shuddering
falling-to-bits buses with people who had to
suffer that all life long
for a pittance — at least
he paid me well, and I could leave —
to that high, airy office with such a vantage over
the noisy, beautiful, grasping, lickerish, gallant,
irresistible city
                hating
having to serve big business but worst of all
proud admanship Oh
how innocent even they
were then
                compared to now
when their child-abuse and youth-abuse
conquer the small screen every brainwashed evening

but Enriqueta was nearly always there
to briefly crisply shake my hand to welcome
me in to the hateful office it almost seemed
like a real welcome she was so
neat and clean and civilized but never
indiscreet nor never
put a word wrong in the wrong
earshot then one day
she took our courage in her hands and showed me
the big book she was reading:

El Crist de nou crucificat
Christ recrucified her own book
in her own tongue I'll never forget
the pride in her eyes in her quiet voice
telling me Salas had done it straight
from Greek not second-hand. She lent it to me
a heavy book to swelter home with but
I juked into the not-quite-nearest pub
and over a cheap, rotgut glass
began to read, soon knowing her right:
for here was Catalan as crisp and rich as
Rovira i Virgili,
                    Auziàs,
                              Sabaz —
though Franco was still
crucifying Christ for years to come.

I kept it far too long but gave it back when
I could not stand bleak admanship no longer
but all that year-or-so of trudging
to boost the adman I kept looking forward
to competent kindness. They'd have kept me
waiting a month for payment,
she knew my need and forced
cash on delivery. While I waited
for ten minutes or half-an-hour
in that bleak dazzling office I sometimes thought
of men who'd never see their country again
because they loved it as much as Enriqueta.
I never spoke to her of them,
there wasn't time — perhaps no need —
perhaps she knew
exiles at home,
neither in exile nor at home.

When competent kindness wasn't there, I'd leave
down-in-the-mouth, the nearest pub with tick
half-an-hour's weary walk away I never
summoned the courage to ask her out for a drink
just as well no doubt but Enriqueta
Enriqueta Bru
you were as crisp and lovely as
you were even finer
than your lovely name.

A Girl in Jerez de la Frontera, in the Autumn of 1952

Lank brownish hair,
and from under a pale-grey shift
only a faint
breast-sign;
her bare limbs thin, limp,
and the oldest face I ever saw,
the most hopeless,
scored by misery,
no gleam at all in her eyes.

Standing in the barber-shop doorway as I was leaving,
she asked me if I wanted her.
I asked how much.

'Un duro,' a five-peseta coin —
the rate was 160 to the pound.

I asked her age.
'Eleven.'

And looking down at her
I believed it.
Poverty, like love, works wonders.

Impeccably, Andalusianly, shaven,
I gave her some money —
can't remember exactly
but not much more than a duro —
and made for the nearest bar.

Duro is slang for a coin.
In the dictionary duro means hard.

Pilgrim

An old, blind, grey-haired, black pilgrim,
his left hand gripping a staff his own height,
almost as if planting it,
his garment grey-and-white,
                              leaving bare
a strong left shoulder. He stands —
with his back to the dream's gaze —
framed in the frame of a door
but there's no door,
                        only that iron rectangle
the pilgrim is standing in, the dream
has no notion of where he has come through,
how long he's been standing there —
as if gazing out
over the vast whitegrey desert in front,
the endless desert —
and that was all there was to the dream:
no movement,
                        a still picture
that seemed to last forever.

That was months ago, now looking back
the man who dreamt it can still see,
as clearly as in that night,
beggar perhaps and pilgrim —
no begging-bowl, no scallop-shell — an old black,
strong, blind man
standing free of iron,
alone, gripping a staff.

Notes

page 14 She fell asleep in the sun: I owe this expression to the poet and scholar Dáithí Ó hÓgáin, who found it for me in the archives of Roinn Bhéaloideas Éireann (the Department of Irish Folklore), University College, Dublin. For that and for other things in the same context I'm grateful to him, as I am to Áine McEvoy (the woman from Kerry) who gave me that incomparable phrase 'leanbh ón ngréin', and to my friend from Tiernahilla (Co Limerick), the poet Pádraig de Vál, for the line 'garsúinín beag mishtake'.

page 16 Een fenster is alles = a window is all. The Flemish poet Paul van Ostaijen was born in 1896 and died in 1928.

page 33 This poem is for Paddy Joe Hill, because on that memorable day in 1991 when the Birmingham Six finally came out of court vindicated one of the first things he said to the world was: 'It's English justice, not British — we can't blame the Scots or the Welsh'.

page 46 Pulcherrima paradigmata = resplendent paradigms. A phrase remembered from Erigena. I couldn't resist it.

page 50 La vella plata = the old silver. The Catalan poet Salvador Espriu used it to mean the Catalan language.